DRIVE THRU

THE ROAD TO

RICE

By Shalini Vallepur

THE RICE BOWL

BEARPORT
PUBLISHING

Minneapolis, Minnesota

Library of Congress Cataloging-in-Publication Data

Names: Vallepur, Shalini, author.
Title: The road to rice / by Shalini Vallepur.
Description: Fusion edition. | Minneapolis, MN : Bearport Publishing
  Company, [2021] | Series: Drive thru | Includes bibliographical
  references and index.
Identifiers: LCCN 2020010638 (print) | LCCN 2020010639 (ebook) | ISBN
  9781647473235 (library binding) | ISBN 9781647473280 (paperback) | ISBN
  9781647473334 (ebook)
Subjects: LCSH: Rice—Juvenile literature.
Classification: LCC SB191.R5 V27 2021 (print) | LCC SB191.R5 (ebook) |
  DDC 633.1/8—dc23
LC record available at https://lccn.loc.gov/2020010638
LC ebook record available at https://lccn.loc.gov/2020010639

For more information, write to Bearport Publishing, 5357 Penn Avenue South, Minneapolis, MN 55419. Printed in the United States of America.

CONTENTS

HOP IN THE RICE BOWL

Welcome to my food truck, the Rice Bowl! My name is Mina, and I make the best rice dishes around. What would you like to eat?

* MENU *

Sushi

White rice bowl

Brown rice bowl

Oh, no! I've run out of rice! I need some more. Hop in the Rice Bowl, and let's get on the road to rice!

THE ROAD TO RICE

Rice grass

Rice grows all over the world except in Antarctica. Rice is a **grain** that comes from a type of grass.

THE RICE BOWL

There are over 40,000 types of rice!

Basmati

Wild

Jasmine

Long brown

Risotto

Sushi

Rice grains come in three different lengths: long, medium, and short. I use short-grain rice. It gets sticky when cooked, which makes it perfect for sushi!

PERFECT WEATHER

Rice grows best in warm places that get a lot of rain and sun. Rice grows on a type of field called a paddy.

Rice paddy, Thailand

Paddies are fields that have been flooded with water.

THE RICE BOWL

First, a rice paddy is **plowed**. Then, the paddy is flooded. **Seedlings** grow in beds before being planted in the rice paddy.

Plowing can be done with a **machine** or with the help of animals.

THE PADDY

These workers are planting seedlings in a flooded paddy.

We made it to the rice paddy! Rice seedlings are planted when they are 30 days old.

THE RICE BOWL

It takes about three to six months for the plants to grow. The rice paddy stays flooded with water while rice grows.

HARVEST

The paddy is drained before the **harvest** begins. Then, workers cut the rice **stalks** using tools called sickles.

Harvesting rice by hand is very hard work.

SICKLE

Combine harvester

Sometimes machines are used to harvest rice quickly. They make harvesting rice easier.

THE RICE BOWL

DRIED AND MILLED

After the harvest, workers dry the rice. This helps the rice last longer. After that, the rice is stored.

Rice might be stored in a place like this.

Then, rice is **milled** to remove layers from the grains of rice. The grains of rice are rubbed together very quickly. This takes off the outer layers of rice.

Layers of rice

ALL TYPES OF RICE

Brown rice still has some of the outer layers. They are good for us.

Brown rice has a lot of **nutrients** and **fiber**.

When all the layers are removed from rice, the rice becomes a white color. This is white rice.

Outer layers

White rice

THE HISTORY OF RICE

Rice is a **staple food** for about half of the world. But where did rice come from? People first started eating rice in China about **10,000** years ago.

China

India

Rice spread from China to India and then across the rest of the world.

Today, there are thousands of types of rice. Jasmine rice and basmati rice are just two examples.

JASMINE RICE

BASMATI RICE

Jasmine rice is short and sticky. Basmati rice is long and dry.

A WORLD OF RICE

Whether it's time for breakfast, lunch, or dinner, rice makes the perfect meal!

Congee is a rice dish ▶ eaten in some Asian countries at breakfast.

CONGEE

◀ Jollof rice comes from West Africa. It is spicy!

JOLLOF

Mochi is a chewy, ▶
sweet rice cake
from Japan.

MOCHI

◀ Rice pudding
from the United
Kingdom is usually
served with jam.

RICE PUDDING

RICE TIME!

We traveled on the road to rice and made it back with lots of rice. Would you like to eat some?

THE RICE BOWL

* MENU *

Sushi

White
rice bowl

Brown
rice bowl

In some Asian languages, the word for rice is a lot like the words used for food and meal. Rice is a very important food!

GLOSSARY

fiber parts of some foods that take longer for the human body to break down

grain the seeds from plants such as wheat and rice that are often used as food

harvest the picking of food crops

machine a thing with moving parts that does work when it is given power

milled when the outer layers of a grain of rice are removed

nutrients important parts of food that animals and plants need to grow

plowed when soil has been turned over

seedlings very young plants

stalks long, thin parts of a plant

staple food a food that is important and eaten a lot

INDEX